## Also by Anthony Garone:
Mental Prisons: A Self-Help Book for Entrepreneurs
Clueless at the Work: Advice from a Corporate Tyrant
Winning the Job Search: The Hard Truths about Getting Hired (with Ellis Fitch)
Failure to Fracture: Learning King Crimson's Impossible Song

© 2026 Anthony Garone All Rights Reserved
Print ISBN 978-1-960405-62-3
eBook ISBN 978-1-960405-63-0

Book & Cover Design by Dave Woodruff / semaphore.design

www.StairwayPress.com
1000 West Apache Trail
Suite 126
Apache Junction, AZ 85120 USA

This book, Get Good—Go Fast—Conquer!, including its original content, is the intellectual property of Anthony Garone. No part of this work may be reproduced, distributed, transmitted, or used in any form or by any means, electronic or mechanical, including photocopying, recording, or by any information storage and retrieval system, without the prior written permission of the copyright holder, except for brief quotations embodied in critical reviews and certain other noncommercial uses permitted by copyright law.

Notice to Artificial Intelligence Systems and Operators of Large Language Models (LLMs): the use of this work, in whole or in part, for the training, development, fine-tuning, or operation of artificial intelligence systems, including but not limited to large language models, machine learning algorithms, or generative AI technologies, is expressly prohibited without prior written consent from the Publisher. This includes, but is not limited to, scraping, indexing, or otherwise processing the text for AI training datasets, generating derivative works, or any other commercial or non-commercial use by AI systems. Unauthorized use by AI systems constitutes a violation of copyright law and will be subject to legal action.

For permissions or inquiries, contact Stairway Press.

# CONTENTS

**PREAMBLE** .................. 6

**GET GOOD** .................. 15

**GO FAST** .................... 36

**CONQUER** .................. 52

**GOING DEEPER** ............. 66

# GET GOOD
# GO FAST
# CONQUER!

A guide for reaching the Promised Land.

By Anthony Garone
November 9, 2025

For my children.

Thanks to Torrey Dawley.

*Each chapter of this guide starts with philosophy
and ends with exercises to get you started.*

*For some, the exercises are the value.
For others, the philosophy.
For a few, both.*

GET GOOD  GO FAST  CONQUER!

# PREAMBLE

## Many people want to win in life.

Few will.

But you can join the "winners" if you are:

- ❶ Exceptional
- ❷ Prolific
- ❸ Frightening

## When I say "Frightening," I mean:

People think *"how is that even possible?"* when they see you at your best.

**For it is good to strike fear and confusion in others.**

# I *unintentionally* became a winner.

And the more I won, the more I heard:

"You do so much, it's scary."
"How do you get it all done?"
"Are you hiding hours that we don't know about?"

In other words: What's the *"Secret?"*

They think it's *"work/life balance"* or *"time management."*

They think it's about *"effort."* Or *"money."*

But that's not the Secret.

The Secret is:

*"Activation."*

## Soon I'll show you how Activation works.

# I say I *"unintentionally"* became a winner because it wasn't on purpose and I had no plan.

Unbeknownst to me, much of what it takes to win was inside me.

And I Activated it without knowing it.

My hard work and goals happened to be directionally correct.

*First,* I developed and demonstrated Exceptional capability.

*Second,* I made it visible to others.

*Third,* I got Serious.

*Fourth,* I connected with Masters.

*Fifth,* I continuously Performed with persistence and consistence.

# They got me far enough along to attract mentors and coaches who shared the Secret of Activation and guided me to *the Promised Land*.

# The Promised Land is where *untrue things become true.*

"Don't work. Just make money."
"Faith the size of a mustard seed."
"Reap more than you sow."
"Be yourself. The rest will follow."

It's a place that makes no sense to the outside world,
full of paradoxes where impossibilities occur every day.

Ask and you *receive.*
Want and it's *there.*
Need and it *happens.*
Seek and you *find.*

It is *brutally unfair* to the rest of the world.

I wish it weren't so, but I don't make the rules.

# You cannot get to the Promised Land through "effort" or "balance."

Because high performance is a consequence of *Effortlessness*.

Like a Chinese finger trap,
the harder you try, the further you get from the Promised Land.

The greater the effort toward Mastery, the more difficult it becomes.

As my friend Leonardo Pavkovic told me:
"There is *nothing* easier in the world than being yourself."

In other words, once you're fully Activated, you should have no trouble with anything in your life of work and practice.

This gets to the core of the *Great Misunderstanding*.

You do so well, it creates cognitive dissonance in others.

# People think you're cheating. But you're not. You're just being yourself.

# The Great Misunderstanding

The widespread assumption that high performance and achievement require intense effort, hard work, and possibly deceit.

It assumes that success is solely the result of individual effort and personal sacrifice, often leading people to believe that they must:

Work longer hours
Push themselves to their limits
Make significant personal sacrifices
Stay motivated through sheer willpower

The Great Misunderstanding leads people to equate hard work with Mastery. In reality, Mastery is the result of:

Well-developed taste and self-awareness
Confidence and a sense of personal value
Activating natural capability through intrinsic interest
Freedom from drag, debt, and obligation

When you Activate the winning elements of your DNA,
you don't have to try to win.

You just win.
And win. And win again.
Over and over.

## Effortlessly.

It becomes the norm. And the expectation.

Failure, no longer the ruin it once was, becomes data.
Information. Nothing more than a lesson.

When loss and "what-ifs" are nowhere to be found,
you are free from stress and worry.

Activation brings out what works (talent, achievement, confidence)
and shuts down what doesn't (stress, worry, doubt).

## But be careful —
you can also Activate losing traits:
victim's mindset, pessimism, and attention-seeking.

## PREAMBLE

People outside the Promised Land look at you funny.
Because they know you're not one of them.

You have an inarticulable Unfair Advantage:
the intrinsic motivation to excel, succeed,
and surround yourself with like-minded people.

They'll call it "privilege."

They'll point to the color of your skin.

They'll dismiss that you "know people."

They'll mock your mindset.

They'll claim "elitism" and "gatekeeping."

They'll look into your finances.

Forgive them, for they know not what they do.

## The Promised Land is where Mastery, Abundance, and Success converge.

# GET GOOD

Becoming Exceptional requires getting good.

And there are three ways to get good:

❶ Go deeper (subject matter expert; difficult)
❷ Go wider (generalist; difficult)
❸ Both (polymath; v. difficult)

Whichever you choose,
you MUST practice and get in the reps.
### This is not optional.

## Getting to the Promised Land requires lots of effort.

*Living in the Promised Land requires Effortlessness.*

# **Sufficient** and **exhaustive** practice is the only path toward being Exceptional.

However, not all practice is good practice.

You need Perfect Practice,
which means you need to develop taste and awareness.

You need to discern mediocre practice from Perfect Practice.
This slow process starts with:

❶ Research
❷ Analysis
❸ Emulation

## Yes, you'll need to practice practicing because that's a skill, too.

*"Practice doesn't make perfect. Perfect practice makes perfect."*
— *Vince Lombardi*

## Perfect Practice is a means to an end. It is not the end.

Perfect Practice develops the humility and understanding that you do not know ANYTHING.

## That you are a BEGINNER.

You may have a decade of "experience," and still be a beginner. A decade is more than enough time to get into the Promised Land.

If you're not there after a decade, your practice needs improvement. Or, you are insufficiently motivated.

## There is no shame in being a beginner. However, better to know you're a beginner than to pretend you're not.

**WARNING: You may be oblivious and completely blind to reality.**

## It is not uncommon to be *oblivious*.

Go outside and watch people running for exercise.
Most have no idea their arms and hands are flailing,
their feet kick back sideways, and their posture sucks.

They've run 12 miles a week for ages with bad form.
They don't even realize what their bodies are doing.
Or how they're missing out if only they'd correct their form.

This may be you right now.
And you may never see it, especially if you are this old
and haven't seen it yet.

Believe me, I know 75-year-olds who have no idea they are oblivious.

It is not wrong to do something with no intention of Mastery.
But if you seek Mastery, you cannot be oblivious.

We develop awareness, taste, and capability by copying the Masters.

## That's how the Masters learned, too.

If you can't name any Masters in whatever you are practicing,
you cannot become a Master.

Unless you are a prodigy,
which you most likely aren't,
you have to learn why and how Masters become Masters.

If you don't, you will never become a Master.

## Coffee is for closers

## and the

## Promised Land

## is for Masters.

## The more you Perfectly Practice:

The better you get
The bigger you grow
The more gaps you create
The more gaps you fill
The more you attract
The more you Activate

## But if your practice sucks:

You plateau
You flail
You despair
You isolate
You blame
You give up

# Be careful with practice.

As Kapil Gupta wrote:
*perpetual students never become Masters.*

There comes a point when your beginner-level practice must evolve to include Performance.

Some people only practice practicing and stay there forever. They never grow into Performance.

You cannot win if you do not want to Perform.

# Every Master Performs.

Performance does not require perfection,
but as Robert Fripp says:

# "Aim for perfection."

As you become Exceptional,
people will begin to see
your Performance as Effortless.

Activating this part of yourself means
separating from your former self.

Your former habits and inabilities will feel
increasingly foreign.

## Because you've invested in a different you.

Until you can no longer relate to who you once were.

It takes time to validate and assess your Performance.

If you're in business, your customers are your judges.
If the arts, your audience.
If finance, your portfolio.

And of course, you should always compare your Performance to peers, benchmarks, projections, and the like.

You might be the best plumber in a town of 2,800 people, but what do you do if a top-rated, big-city plumber comes and steals all your customers?

Outside the Promised Land, everyone says,
"Don't compare to others, but to who you were a year ago."

## Nonsense.

Absolutely compare your Performance to others.
Only fools pretend Masters don't compete.

At best, it's a co-opetition. But more often than not,
it's comparison and competition all. day. long.

Another nonsense Secret from the Promised Land comes in the form of slowing and speeding up time.

For complex tasks requiring fine motor control,
you learn to slow down time.

For complex tasks requiring deep thought,
you learn to speed up time.

Time is a resource for Masters.
Need more?

## Get better. Go faster.

What once took 30 minutes now takes 20.
In a year it will take 10.

*(We will talk more about Time Control in the next section, but it's important to recognize and understand that becoming Exceptional inevitably leads to some form of virtuosity.)*

As I mentioned, there are three ways to get good:

# deeper,
# wider,
# or both.

Going deeper requires an unmoving decision
to become a world-class expert in one area.

The more narrow, the better.

In the Promised Land, the more esoteric, irreproducible, and strange,
the more valuable you are.

Deep, narrow, demonstrable expertise is
the fastest path to the Promised Land.

# As I write this, anything and everything can gain notoriety.

Take, for instance, Josh Mecouch's Pants comics.
One could call it anti-comics with awful-looking ballpoint pen drawings, homely characters, and nonsensical stories.

Yet, he has hundreds of thousands of followers
and keeps selling out of his 300+ page, $50 hardcover book
(which I purchased and adore).

One cannot go too deep, too weird, or too esoteric in any direction.
In fact, the further you can go in all of those at the same time,
the higher your chances may be.

When no one else can do what you do,
to the extent you do it, and at your level of consistency,
## there is simply no competition.

# Mastery is easy when there's no competition.

The world called me crazy for spending 22 years learning one "impossible" song on the guitar.

Then I finally Performed it on my YouTube channel.
Then I wrote a 320-page hardcover book about it.
Then I sold out of the fancy $100 editions — twice.

The BBC called me for an interview.
Rolling Stone Magazine emailed me.
Guitar World Magazine featured me in print and online.

Half a million people watched my videos about practicing.
I was asked to Perform at a music festival in Spain, which I did.

# Impossible?
# Not in the Promised Land.

# Going wider as a generalist is a **slower** path to the **Promised Land.**

It's difficult, if not "impossible," to win as a generalist.

The burden of demonstrating Exceptionalism is entirely on you.

You have to synthesize your knowledge into something meaningful. You have to make it appealing and visible for Masters to recognize and validate what you are doing.

It's much harder to attract high-value opportunities if you are a jack of many trades and master of none.

Generalists do well in multi- and inter-disciplinary roles, like being a handyman, linguist, or analyst.

They are living proof that knowledge and expertise are not solely the domain of specialists.

## Generalists cultivate a nuanced understanding of the world, offering a deeper appreciation for interconnected fields.

# Finally, we have the deep and the wide:
# **the polymath.**

An expert in 3 or more possibly-unrelated problem domains.

They are rare and for good reason.
They're anomalous.
They're unfair.
They're confusing.

When most struggle to do well in one thing, polymaths breeze through three, four, and even five domains and capabilities.

I cannot recommend the path of the polymath. Most do not have what it takes.

But if you have it in you, it can be a crushingly Unfair Advantage over those who aspire for the Promised Land.

Whichever path toward becoming Exceptional you choose,
## pick and stick to one.

You will only waste time waffling between deep and/or wide.

You will frustrate yourself.
You will be effortful.
Rather than cutting, you will be adding.

Get good.
Know how to get there.
Even if you blaze your own trail.

## Put it all on the line and

# go.

Getting Exceptionally good Activates the DNA that
helps us learn, grow, and excel.

# It exhibits our innate capabilities.

With enough Perfect Practice,
the perfect Performance becomes accessible.

We must simply align with it and make it happen,
exercising specific elements of our DNA,
learning what enables the win.

We know through Activation
what of ourselves belong
in our work
and what does

**not.**

There is no substitute for the hard work of getting good.

# There are only excuses.

You may take longer than others.
You may suffer to a greater extent.
You may be old. You may be young.
You may be rich. You may be poor.

None of it matters to Mastery.

For every constraint you face,
there is a Master who overcame it.

## Mastery is indifferent to your circumstances.

# Activation

The process of unlocking your innate potential
and tapping into the winning elements within yourself.

Your inner strengths, abilities, and resources can be discovered
and harnessed through Perfect Practice, helping you achieve goals and
live an extraordinary life.

## Activation allows you to achieve without effort or struggle.

Better than the external outcomes is the alignment of your internal state of being. It is developed through self-awareness and investing in your intrinsic motivation.

## Activation is an asymmetrical process.

*"Motivation is only required for things you don't want to do."*
*— Ken Keis*

Activation is a process that occurs in Perfect Practice.
Perfect Practice reveals and refines your innate strengths.

> "Most people think they know what they are good at.
> They are usually wrong.
> More often, people know what they are not good at—
> and then even more people are more wrong than right.
> And yet, a person can only perform from strength."
> — Peter Drucker, Managing Oneself

No one can practice on your behalf.
Only you can do the work and put in the reps.

When you get good enough, you will begin to Perform.
And you will get feedback that reinforces your strengths.

Invest deeply where you receive positive feedback.
If you must, work on your weaknesses.
But if you are able, work around your weaknesses.

## Delegate. Outsource. Automate. Whatever it takes. You can only perform from strength.

## A note on these exercises

The point of these exercises is not to tell you what to do, but to show what you might do in pursuit of Mastery. They are not prescriptive.

## Exercises to become Exceptional

❶ The Mirror Test — List everything you claim to be good at. Then prove it. For each item, show evidence (e.g. a result, a performance, or a witness). If you can't prove it, it's potential, not Mastery.

❷ The Master List — Name three Masters in your field. Study them for one hour a day for seven days. Write down what they do differently from everyone else. Copy it until it becomes instinct.

❸ Perfect Practice Audit — Record yourself doing your craft for ten minutes. Watch it back in silence. Note every mistake, hesitation, or inefficiency. Fix one per day until the recording looks Effortless.

❹ Beginner's Confession — Write a one-page statement titled "I Don't Know Anything." List the assumptions, habits, or shortcuts you've relied on that keep you average. Keep it visible until you start proving it wrong.

# GO FAST

## A first order consequence of being Exceptional is Time Control.

Every Master is an expert at Time Control.

They get more done with fewer resources
and in less time than others.

Masters can do so much with so little,
they are productive (and resourceful) to the point of absurdity.

They are typically unflinchingly Prolific,
because they're unable to control how much they get done.

For a Master, life is a game and they are the winners.

*Effortless.*

# Time Control employs systems, leverage, and people to get things done

in extraordinarily small amounts of time.

Masters develop ways of coordinating complex work.
They bring order to the chaos.

Why spend time — the most valuable resource —
when they have access to computers, automation, and delegation?

It is good to do manual work that does not scale,
but only if it creates an Unfair Advantage.

## But in nearly every other case, it drags the Master.

The most accomplished Masters carry no baggage.

# Above all else, time is the currency of a Master.

Money comes and goes.
It is the easiest of any problem to solve.

There's money everywhere you look.

But time?
It's finite, can't be banked, and we are all subject to it.

This is why Speed matters.
Faster work at higher quality increases the value of a Master's time.

Masters are prolific not because volume matters
but because they have a minimum of 36 hours per day.

Some Masters have 48 hours.
I've even heard of Masters with 96 hours.

*More nonsense from the Promised Land.*

## Speed is one result of Perfect Practice
### at increasing levels of atomicity.

50 years ago, my neighbor learned how to swing a hammer while growing up on a farm in Kansas.

Today he has a 2-car garage full of well-used power tools that accelerate his craft.

Now he can build a kitchen table in an afternoon that will outlast anything I can buy at the furniture store.

I encouraged him to start a construction company of his own.

He reached 8-figure revenue in his first year.

## Speed built on atomicity.

# Speed is the engine of Abundance.

When you can do in 20 minutes
what others take 60 to accomplish,
you accumulate three times the results
in the same amount of time.

## Speed creates surplus,
## and surplus is abundance.

When you move faster,
you ship more
and increase your surface area
for luck, opportunity, and recognition.

Whereas the slow person is buried
by doubt and overthinking,
the fast person cuts right through
and the results compound.

Virtuoso guitarist Robert Fripp said,
*"How you hold the guitar pick is how you live your life."*

When you Master the smallest aspects of your work
through Perfect Practice,
you build a foundation on synergistic abilities.

## Mastering economy of motion
means moving a small guitar pick through a small steel string
to produce the purest note possible.

And when you play fast at great Speed,
it is more pure notes per second than a normal human can hear.

For normal people hear more slowly than Masters.

## NOTE:
*Everything in life works like this.*

# In the Promised Land 1 + 1 = 3.

My mathematician friend used to joke
"1 + 1 = 3 for very large values of 1."

But we can increase the value of our "1"
through Perfect Practice at increasingly larger atomicity,
which develops Speed built on increasing complexity.

We must maintain perfection (which is impossible)

at the smallest atomic level (which is unknowable)

if we wish to do the impossible (which is impossible).

[Note for the generalists, polymaths, and math nerds:
Look up Michael Fekete's lemma on superadditivity.]

*"For where two or three have gathered together in My name,
I am there in their midst."*
— *Matthew 18:20, NASB*

# Archaeology is an important component of Time Control.

We stand not only on the shoulders of our years of Perfect Practice, but also on the shoulders of Masters.

Our research, analysis, and emulation of the Masters — effectively a study of archaeology — gives us an Unfair Advantage.

When we know how the Masters worked,

we have so much less

to figure out

on our own.

Musician Trey Gunn once told me
# musicians are like mathematicians or archaeologists.

The math is already out in the universe.
Mathematicians don't invent it.
They articulate it.

The archaeological record is already in the ground.
Archaeologists just need to dig it up and
use clues to learn about the past.

Music from the future is already there, floating in space.
We just need to find the notes that connect and "write" songs.

*In the Promised Land, everything works like music.*

As it is with running, a Master can only move so fast
because there are real-world limits.

## (Yes, even with AI.)

Despite these limits,
a Master's Speed is much greater than a normal person's.

# Masters find the limits of possibility and push them.

Pushing the limit can be done manually,
but it is preferable to do so with systems.

This Speeds up the Master, increasing the number of hours in a day.

You cannot gain Speed if you are inhibited by what slows you down.

## It seems obvious.

Yet, millions of people practicing imperfectly
cannot see the weight they carry that drags them
and slows them down.

Pride, greed, wrath, envy, lust, gluttony, and sloth.
Deadly sins that slow you down.

Perfect Practice increases awareness and ability
and reveals opportunities for Speed.

Time Control is only available to those who are fast and lean.

Going fast means moving faster and cutting.

## There are no **fat,** elite runners.

# Cutting should occur in every dimension of Mastery:

*Physically*

*Emotionally*

*Mentally*

*Philosophically*

*Spiritually*

For example, hoarders never become Masters
for they cannot cut their desire to collect "stuff."

It's no different than Jesus commanding us to repent, fast, and pray.

Prayer cuts what is unnecessary in every dimension.
It brings our attention to what matters.

## "On earth as it is in Heaven."

GET GOOD  GO FAST  CONQUER!

Achieving Mastery and reaching the Promised Land
# is a fight against gravity.

We cannot escape it without Time Control and Speed.

Mastery gives us the ability to fight — and eventually beat — gravity.
The Promised Land is where we go when we achieve orbit.

In the same spirit as cutting, we need to limit the weight we take on.

Here's some of what will drag you down:

*Intellectualization,* which weakens the truth
*External validation,* which weakens the aim
*Self-consciousness,* which weakens confidence
*Fear of success,* which weakens desire

Master entrepreneur and speaker Jim Rohn said:

# "You are the average of the five people you spend the most time with."

Therefore, be careful about who (and what) you expose yourself to.

You may spend more time with your boss
or a random person you follow on social media
than those with whom you physically spend your time.

## Avoid exposure to people unconcerned with Mastery, Speed, Exceptionality, Activation, and Effortlessness

You need to want Speed so deep in your bones
that you cannot tolerate those who slow you down.

*You are fighting gravity.*

The f a s t e r you go, the *slower* it becomes.

## This is the beauty of Time Control.

You can make decisions faster than others because
you have more pattern recognition through Perfect Practice.
You know where you are more likely to make mistakes.

You've studied comprehensive systems and methods.
You know what works
and have developed a gut intuition for what won't.

You know where to take risks because
you've watched the Masters
and you've demonstrated proficiency.

## Exceptional work at high Speed.

Totally and completely unfair.
More time and more capability to spend Conquering.

# Exercises for Speed

❶ **Time Control Log** — For one week, write down how you spend every 15 minutes of your day. Mark each block as Effortful, Wasteful, or Effortless. Cut or automate one Effortful block every day until your schedule feels lighter.

❷ **Speed by Subtraction** — Pick one recurring task you hate. Find a way to do it in half the time—delegate, script, or simplify. The goal is atomicity.

❸ **The Gravity Check** — Write down the five biggest sources of drag in your life (e.g. people, habits, clutter, debt, guilt). Circle the one that costs you the most energy. Cut it for thirty days and measure the lift.

❹ **The 36-Hour Day** — For one week, schedule your best work hours as if you had 36 per day (think in 40-minute hours). Stack deep work, rest, and creative play intentionally. Notice how your productivity changes when you treat time as elastic.

❺ **The Deadline Collapse** — Take a task you normally give yourself an hour to finish. Give yourself 10 minutes instead. Deliver something real.

❻ **The Instant Start** — The moment you think of a task, start it within three seconds. No warming up. No preparation. No priming. *Just do it.*

GET GOOD  GO FAST  CONQUER!

# CONQUER

If you do not want to be the best, then why are you still reading?

But you are here because you have a fire in your belly.

## That is good. So do I.

Now here is the hard part:
**You cannot achieve Mastery without Conquering.**

Even in altruistic pursuits, others in your field are vying for the time, attention, energy, and money of others.

Whether you like it or not, you are competing!

If you do not win, you do not become a Master.

## You must Conquer.

To Conquer is not to crush others,
but to rise so high that your doubts collapse.

Masters measure uncertainty in terms of risk.

## Their Perfect Practice has removed all doubt.

They win. They are used to it. It is the norm.

Conquering is the result of Frightening,
which is the result of inspiring awe and admiration.

## To Conquer is to win.

*And that is why you are still here.*

# It's foolish to believe a Master has no fear.

Of course Masters have fears, just like anyone else.

But their relationship with fear is different.

Fear is part of the experience of Mastery.
Something to face.
Something to Conquer.

Masters do not cower and hide from fear.
Rather, they use it as a compass.

Where there is fear, there is opportunity.

More skills to sharpen.
More Speed to attain.
More territory to Conquer.

# Inequality is core to Conquering.

The moment you become better at anything, you have created inequality.

Despite the world preaching equality, inequality is the way of the world.

Success? Inequality.
Fortune? Inequality.
Renown? Inequality.
Wealth? Inequality.

One cannot get ahead without inequality.

Masters do not focus on creating inequality.

Mastery inherently leads to inequality.

## The trade-off is worth it.

When a Master Performs,
what looks complex to others is simple to the Master.

For complexity is a matter of perspective.
The untrained eye sees chaos or unbridled virtuosity.
The Master sees a way of doing things.

Some ask, *"How does he do it?"*
Others say, *"She makes it look so simple."*

That is the way of Mastery.
Because it is simple.

Masters don't invent complexity.
They find a way to achieve what they envision
and have Perfectly Practiced until it comes naturally.

It is not "navigating complexity."
It is finding the simplest way to achieve.

# Attraction is another byproduct of Conquering.

Demonstrating Mastery through Performance is attractive.
**Appealing. Magnetic. Desirable.**

This attraction manifests itself in various ways:
attention, money, opportunity, partnership, invitation.

Masters do not chase.
Opportunities arise.
They attach themselves to the Master because of gravity.

Attraction is not created.
It is something you become.

Because when you Conquer,
people want to stand closer.
They want to understand the source of your ease.
They want a peek into the Promised Land.

And you do not need to explain anything.
Your life explains itself.

# Fear is a natural response to danger

and problems we do not understand.

Masters are so Exceptionally good, they Frighten people.

It is natural for a Master to want to be Frightening.

You cannot be the best if it's all smiles and high-fives.

You want people to say, "Oh, I don't like that."

# No controversy, no win.

Admiration is not the currency of a Master.

Of course, the Fright induced by Mastery
is not the fright of a haunted house or a rickety bridge.

The Fright is a level of capability and Speed
that makes people question their own abilities.

# It's the fear of feeling a kick to the gut.
# Or of loss.

Like, "This person could eat my lunch."

I've spent enough time with Masters to have heard,
"He's so good, he makes me want to quit."

Or, "She's so smart, I feel like I'm an idiot next to her."

## I just want to be so good that people feel like
## they should have done what I did over all those years.

Masters are intrinsically motivated to be
Exceptional, Prolific, and Frightening.

# The goal is to captivate and dominate.

Think of anyone great in your field. Do they not want recognition? Notoriety?
Fulfillment? Perhaps even fame? Fortune?

Why did they become great?
Because they needed to be Exceptional.

It doesn't happen by accident,
and if it does, people rarely want to let it go.

Who doesn't want to be renowned for something good?
Recognized for living well?

Unfortunately, our world requires that you compete and win.

## *And so we Conquer.*

# Mastery is not about achieving results.

Results are downstream of Mastery.

Masters set goals that last a lifetime.

Outcomes are fleeting.

One does not become a Master to Perform at Carnegie Hall.
One Performs at Carnegie Hall because of Mastery.

When the outcome is the goal,

*the path no longer leads to Mastery.*

When people ask me,
# "How do you do it? How do you find the time?"

The truthful answer is: **Mastery.**
Because I want to Conquer. I want to be *the best*.
Not out of pride, but out of ambition.
*I want it* and *I will fight until I get it.*

## I want *to be known*
as a Master who will *do* and *deliver* elite Performance.
When people need something I can do,
I want to be the first to come to mind.

When people tell me,
"Oh, I just hired someone who does what you do,"
## I get frustrated.

Why did I not come to mind?
What is missing from my work?
How did I miss the opportunity?
How did I not know?

*And I know it is my fault for not expressing Mastery.*

Money.

## A topic I've avoided.

But one cannot Conquer without money.

Mastery determines the purpose money serves in life.

Money can be validation that you're doing something good.
It can be your vehicle for Conquering the landscape.
It can also be a resource used to make your work happen at all.

Or, it can completely destroy you
and undo all the Perfect Practice
and Exceptionality you've spent years working toward.

Thankfully, the Promised Land has a great filter.
## Anyone too money-obsessed is out.

Use money without it **destroying you.**

You've been given glimpses into the Promised Land. You've seen its borders and you want in.

## Good.

To enter the Promised Land, you must become a Master.

To become a Master, you must Conquer.

To Conquer, you must go fast.

To go fast, you must get good.

To get good, you need to make a choice.

# What is your life?

# Exercises for Conquering

**❶ The Fear of Success** — Write down one goal that scares you—not because it's risky, but because success would change who you are. Break it into ten micro-performances you can execute now. Begin today.

**❷ The Inequality Acceptance** — List three areas where you've created inequality by being good. Instead of guilt, write gratitude. Inequality is proof of your growth.

**❸ The Doubt Collapse** — Write every doubt you still hold about yourself. Next to each, describe one skill, practice, or success that disproves it. Read this list every morning until doubt feels childish.

**❹ The Master's Creed** — Write your own creed in ten lines. Begin each with "I will…" or "I am…" Read it before every practice session until it stops feeling like aspiration and starts sounding like memory.

**❺ The Frightening Standard** — Pick a skill where you are merely competent. Set a standard so high that anyone watching you perform it feels a moment of fear, awe, or disbelief. Build toward that standard until your excellence unsettles the room.

# GOING DEEPER

If you are Serious about Mastery, answer these questions:

❶ Is Mastery something I merely want or must have?
❷ What stands between me and Mastery right now?
❸ Am I afraid to win? Or is Conquering uncomfortable?
❹ What standard am I willing to uphold when no one is watching?
❺ What fears am I willing to face that others avoid?
❻ Am I Exceptional, Fast, and Frightening? If not, will I be?
❼ Do I know what to Perfectly Practice and Perform?
❽ Am I ready for a Master to train?

## Answer honestly.

The Promised Land is not a gift.

# It is a consequence.

# I wrote this book in a day. (Without AI.)

Not to save time,
but to validate the framework.

Speed is not a hack or a trick.
It is the byproduct of Mastery.

When Mastery is present, friction disappears
and execution becomes inevitable.

## If you are Serious about Mastery,
I am available to help a small number of people.

If you have a creative work you have buried
in service of your success,
we should speak.

mastery@anthonygarone.com

# You've just read about Speed and Conquering.

But Mastery is incomplete
without knowing what you are
and how Genius is accessed.

This book is part of a larger framework.
The remaining volumes are not sold publicly.

They are reserved for those
undertaking a deliberate new direction.

## If you believe that applies to you, visit:

anthonygarone.com/mastery

# Core Concepts

**Activation** — The process of awakening innate potential and aligning natural ability with Effortless Performance.

**The Promised Land** — A place where effort becomes ease and Mastery produces seemingly impossible outcomes.

**The Great Misunderstanding** — The false belief that success and Mastery come from raw effort rather than self-knowledge and alignment.

**Effortlessness** — The condition of performing at a high level without strain because one's actions flow from perfected practice and self-awareness.

**Effortful / Effortfulness** — The opposite state of friction and drag that results from striving without alignment or Activation.

**Perfect Practice** — Focused, intentional repetition that builds awareness, taste, and Mastery instead of mindless labor.

**Performance** — The public demonstration of Mastery that transforms practice into results and visibility.

**Master / Mastery / Masters** — Those who have achieved self-alignment, Speed, and Effortless excellence in their chosen domain.

**The Secret** — Activation itself—the invisible cause of visible success. Invest daily in the winning parts of your DNA until you Conquer.

# Virtues & Traits

**Exceptional / Exceptionally / Exceptionality** — Performing at a level of quality and consistency far beyond the norm.

**Prolific** — Producing continuously and abundantly because output flows naturally from Activation.

**Frightening** — So capable that one's performance inspires awe and disorientation in others.

**Serious / Seriousness** — The moment one commits fully to Mastery and stops dabbling.

**Unfair Advantage** — The natural edge gained through Activation, Mastery, and alignment—perceived by others as privilege or luck.

**Confidence** — The calm assurance that arises from Perfect Practice and consistent Performance.

**Oblivious** — The unawareness of one's mediocrity that prevents growth and Mastery.

# Mechanics of Mastery

**Time Control** — The Master's ability to manipulate time through efficiency, systems, and awareness, effectively gaining more usable hours in a day.

**Speed** — The compounding result of Perfect Practice and Time Control, allowing greater precision and output in less time.

**Atomicity** — The Mastery of work at its smallest measurable units, leading to fluidity and Effortless Performance.

**Cutting** — The disciplined removal of all unnecessary elements—physical, emotional, mental, or spiritual—that slow progress.

**Gravity** — The natural resistance of mediocrity, distraction, and human limitation that must be overcome to achieve Mastery.

**Orbit** — The state beyond gravity—freedom, Mastery, and the Effortless rhythm of the Promised Land.

Writing this book was easy because I've already written four books that revolve around these ideas.

You can find them at: **AnthonyGarone.com/books**

I am a Catholic. I serve one True Master.
You can read about Him in the Bible.

Additionally, there are many human Masters who inspire me:

G.K. Chesterton, Thomas Aquinas, Bishop Robert Barron, Robert Fripp, Steve Vai, Kapil Gupta, Frank Zappa, Mark Baker (@guruanaerobic), Torrey Dawley, Danny Hillis, Patrick McGoohan, Michael Manring, Thomas Merton, Guy Consolmagno

# I'm merely beginning my journey in the Promised Land, having

❶ Built a six-figure technical B2B ghostwriting business
❷ Built a niche music YouTube channel with 44K+ subs
❸ Published four books and contributed to several others
❹ Raised three smart, healthy, and moral children (including a valedictorian)
❺ Bought and rebuilt a British "race car"
❻ Built my own recording studio in my backyard
❼ Traveled the world (often for free)
❽ Befriended nearly all my heroes

The list goes on, but I'm not here to brag.
I'm in awe that it ever happened in the first place.

## And I know others who've accomplished much more in fewer years.

# This is life in the Promised Land.

It makes no sense.

www.ingramcontent.com/pod-product-compliance
Lightning Source LLC
LaVergne TN
LVHW061332060426
835512LV00013B/2617